A
Movement
of
Light

The Light Poetry Series

Book 1
The Light That Heals

Book 2
A Movement of Light

Book 3
Light in Slow Motion

Book 4
The Memory of Light

A Movement of Light

Keith Wrassmann

AVAILABLE LIGHT PRESS
Maineville, Ohio

Copyright © Keith Wrassmann, 2023

All rights reserved. No part of this book may be reproduced or used in any manner without the prior written permission of the copyright owner, except for the use of brief quotations in a book review.

Printed in the United States of America.

ISBN: 978-1-961631-01-4
ISBN: 978-1-961631-02-1 (ebook)

Library of Congress Control Number: 2023946895

First Edition

Published by Available Light Press, Maineville, Ohio.

www.availablelightpress.com

Visit the author's website at www.keithwrassmann.com

*For Joshua and Isabella—
the joy, the adventure,
the surprise, and the innocence
of love.*

Contents

Illuminate	*15*
Purpose	*16*
Brim	*17*
Self-Forgiveness	*18*
Reckoning	*20*
Majesty	*21*
Renewal	*22*
Endeavor	*24*
Afterwards	*25*
Final Moment	*27*
Awaking	*28*
Journey	*30*
Even This	*31*
Forgiving Others	*32*
Seeing	*34*
Duration	*35*
Here	*36*
Refinement	*38*
Waking	*40*
Brilliant	*41*
Equilibrium	*43*
Look Up Again	*44*
Release	*46*
Insecurity	*48*

Longing	*50*
You Will Move On	*51*
Contentment	*52*
Decision	*54*
Gather Light	*55*
Anger	*57*
Passage	*58*
Design	*60*
Growth	*61*
Refocus	*62*
Refining	*64*
Present Light	*66*
Ocean	*68*
Silence	*69*
Baseline	*71*
Light Eternal	*72*
Don't Quit	*73*
Discovery	*74*
Joy	*75*
Within	*76*
Unknown	*78*
Last Light	*79*
Perfection	*80*
Robin	*82*
Illusion	*84*
Brighten	*85*
Captured	*86*
Creation	*88*

On Desire	*90*
Transcend	*91*
Downpour	*93*
The Regrettable	*95*
Paradigm	*96*
Visible Light	*98*
Seasons	*100*
Grow	*102*
Awareness	*104*
December	*106*
Opportunity	*107*
Between	*109*
Moment	*111*
Choose	*112*
Slower Light	*114*
Descending	*115*
Unveiled	*117*
Ascent	*119*
Union	*121*
After	*123*
A Movement of Light	*125*
Thematic Subject Index	*131*

*Life is for living,
for receiving and giving,
for illuminating the darkness
in moving from here to there.*

A Movement of Light

Illuminate

Dear Soul,
rise and illuminate.
Do not sit in despair.
Pain enchants you with
the slumber of solitude,
but you have ability
to see in the dark.
So rise.
Do not let fear
of what you may experience
dim your trajectory.
You are a movement of light,
both particle and wave
as you focus in and out
of this present illusion.
Shadow cannot alter you
or hide the nature of your brilliant soul.
Rise and
stream through this world
with the pinpoint precision
your intention enables,
engaging and creating
with the spectrum of possibility.
You are the dawn that never dulls,
the sunset that never fades.

Purpose

So much at stake in this light,
in the rising and fading,
the experience of reality
in the state of illusion.
You engage the world
with fascination and expectation
of all you came to learn.
You swell with joy
and deflate with sorrow;
neither is permanent.
But what lasts is what you take in,
what you hold in your soul.
Experience pierces the shell
and remains in the heart.
You transform in the processing,
in the acceptance of the moment.
You deepen in hue,
brighten in radiance,
sharpen in clarity.
Life is for living,
for receiving and giving,
for illuminating the darkness
in moving from here to there.

Brim

When feeling overwhelmed
with human interaction,
the soul desires to retreat
to its own intimate space.
When we have given
to our fullest capacity,
we crave the comfort of silence,
of solitude,
where nothing will put forth a new demand.
The center of the soul is sacred,
an inner healing place
that slows the sand of time to build anew.
And in this inner depth,
we process what we
thought,
said,
and did.
We rest until we brim with golden light.
Then newness comes,
rejuvenation,
regeneration,
to once again engage the shadow world,
to be and become,
to give and receive,
to live.

Self-Forgiveness

You cannot live in the memory
of where you think you failed,
or of what brings you shame.
It colors your movement
through the world
with oppressive hues.
It dulls your confidence
in constantly reminding you
that you are not good enough,
that you are flawed,
that you will just do it again.
Forgiveness is a necessary grace.
Give yourself
the right to make mistakes,
to learn,
to grow,
to change.
You owe yourself
the right to move forward,
to leave behind what you cannot undo.
The world moves on
despite its many flaws.
We do not shame the summer
for losing its light in the end,
for we know it is the mark of change,

that fall shines brightest in the dimming light.
And so it is with you.
Failure is the mark of imminent change.
Shame is the ghost that haunts the wearied soul.
Forgiveness is the dawn that brings back light.

Reckoning

How do you start over
after what you lost,
when life took away
what it so willingly gave?
You sank into the center of yourself,
and the world faded out of view.
And in this space,
you faced the reckoning
of all you hoped your life would bring to pass.
The hardest moments bear the deepest wisdom.
When you are ready,
you will make the journey
back to the familiar self,
though changed,
and face the world once more with guarded hope,
with a heart that longs again
to know the goodness of the world,
its love, beauty, warmth,
its gentleness, positivity, charity,
and to see again the fledgling,
the sprouted seed,
the budding flower.

Majesty

You love looking out over the sea
because it reminds you of
the place from where you came.
But this reason hides from you.
How could you embrace this difficulty
in memory of a more golden light?
The majesty of the sea
reminds you of a time
when you were beyond whole,
when flesh and blood were but a blurry dream.
Back there, you spoke with angels
and watched the universe expand and cool.
But here, you speak to yourself
and try to understand the reasons for life's
pain, sorrow, and hardship.
You love looking out over the sea
because you hear beneath its thunder
the warm and gentle whisper
of who you really are,
and feel the never-ending wind
that blows on the shore,
that brings the waves,
the gull,
and the mist—
salty on your lips.

Renewal

Do not give up,
let go.
You grip the past
as if it holds the secret key
that will fix your problems.
The problem, though,
is you cannot fix the wrongs
with the same thoughts and actions
that created them.
Do not give up,
let go.
Be finished with the way you
feel about it.
Each time you replay the trauma
only continues the pain.
The body relives the hurt
your thoughts impose on it,
over and over again.
Do not give up,
let go.
Find solace in moving forward
instead of hoping for resolve
looking backward.
Your peace waits just ahead,
but you have to find courage

to take the steps to get it.
Do not give up,
let go.
Release yourself from yesterday.
Free your hands from
the memories that haunt you,
so you may grasp
the hope that appears before you,
the promise of healing,
freedom,
love,
like how spring must fight
to waken from its slumber
to once again rebirth the darkened world.

Endeavor

Do not let the challenges of life
scare you into immobility.
Through endeavoring
you bring desire
into reality.
You may not know what to do
at first,
but uncertainty gives way to
familiarity.
All action is learning in motion.
To try and then fail
still brings growth.
Do not fear what expands your understanding,
even if it causes pain or sorrow.
To become is the gift of life.
You will push through.
You are not here to shimmer,
but to illuminate and burn
with the force of a thousand suns.
This is your birthright.

Afterwards

What was it about change
that scared you?
It was the newness and uncertainty
of what life would be like
in the afterwards.
You embraced change
not because you wanted to,
but because you had to.
But you are like the butterfly
that emerges from its chrysalis—
it knows what it is supposed to do
void of any known experience,
except what it carries
in the million years of its genes.
So it rests until it dries.
It stretches its legs.
It unfolds its wings.
It tests the wind and temperature.
When it is ready,
it falls from the leaf
where it slumbered safely through the turbulence,
and then it flies.
It lives the life it never could have lived
while bound to grasses, plants, and tree branches.
It does not look back on the past,

but presses forward on its new adventure,
sometimes erratic,
sometimes still,
in its discovery.
It paints the world with hues that charm the eye,
not by effort or intention,
but by its very nature.

Final Moment

How could you find comfort
on a day like today?—
a day you knew would come,
though you did not want it to.
You envisioned the final moment
a thousand times,
rehearsing how you would feel
and what you would say,
so you would be prepared
and have no regrets.
The final moment
forced you to let go,
as she was forced to let go,
both together but separate,
one drifting toward the golden shore
and the other looking up into the sky.
The fading sun left ripples in its wake
and held her hand to lead her home,
and you, eyes set on the horizon,
took in her final light before the fade,
the last gasp of evening,
the inevitable finality.
In silence is comfort,
in the sunset,
in memory.

Awaking

You fear the death
of the body
because you have forgotten
from where you have come.
The world is but a trick of splendid light
that pries from your soul
the memory of the golden shore.
And though you cannot see it with your eyes,
your heart retains the hope of something more.
But life convinces you with its
pain,
sorrow,
hardship,
devastation,
and struggle
that this is all there is,
that you are all that is,
that when you close your eyes, existence ends.
Your destiny from the beginning
is to believe the lie.
For what is life
without the greatest risk of all,
the greatest fear your consciousness can hold?—
that you end,
that darkness is the inescapable truth.

The fear of death ends
when you pass through it
and return home,
and memory rushes upon you,
like when awaking
from the depth of sleep,
and you remember who you really are.

Journey

Today is a day
of not looking back,
of moving past the part of you
that did not think
it could continue one more moment.
Yesterday was the day
of fear,
of insecurity,
of dwelling on the things that burdened you.
Today is a day
of grasping the power of change,
to heal,
to grow in ways that move you forward.
Your soul remembers
its final destination
and how to find its way back to the light.
It knows the rocky path
is not meant for harm,
but for stumbling and recovering,
for learning,
for discovering who you are
and why you have come.
Shift your perspective on today—
the forever tomorrow—
and find solace in the journey,
and rejoice like morning when night has passed.

Even This

The end came before you
expected it,
before anyone knew
what was happening.
The end was not like
the beginning:
no one brought balloons
or said *congratulations*.
I'm sorry was your consolation prize.
But love is not the less, despite its loss,
the brief but brilliant flash that fades too soon.
Love transcends the pain that living brings,
though harder to see
when the wound is new.
But this will heal,
even this.
And time will wipe your cheek and take your hand,
and walk you out beneath the silver stars,
and gently lift your face toward points of light
that shine and dance against the darkest night,
each star a soul, a blessed memory,
that lives and reigns in its eternal place,
that waits until at last it reunites
with what it left behind
for only but a moment passed in time.

Forgiving Others

When another's words or actions
cause heartache and pain,
we register the offense
in anger and sadness.
We harbor negativity
that brews against the one
who dealt the blow.
How could he do this?
Why did she say that?
Human interaction
is a game of cause and effect
in a world not designed to protect us.
The illusion of separation
grants the license,
and human nature
exploits it to its satisfaction.
Forgive the one who hurt you.
But I can't, you plead,
he doesn't deserve it. I am too hurt.
The light replied,
Forgiving others their offenses
is not for them,
but for you.
Relational resentment
is sickness to the soul.

It does not bring about a resolution,
or offer a solution
for the pain.
Instead, it grows until it becomes
a part of you,
and dims the light of your impassioned heart.
But you are meant for better.
Release yourself from harboring resentment
toward those who harmed you.
Then, your heart will recover its light
like when the morning sun
burns away the heavy mist of night.

Seeing

Love will teach you how to say goodbye.
At first, you will not know how to let go,
for the shock will confront you
and make you think the world is deeply flawed.
And the witness of apparent cruelty
will harden you.
But you will recover.
And from here, you will realize
that leaving is only an illusion,
a sleight of hand
that makes the card disappear.
Though still painful,
it's not what it at first appeared to be.
Through experience, you will
understand the trick.
You will know that life is more
than what you can quantify by sight,
that though you die, you live.
Then death will lose the power of fear.
Goodbye is only temporary.
Love remains,
the bond that endures
beyond this darkened light.

Duration

All the struggle you endure will end,
though you think it won't
in the long duration.
What is your life?—
a wave of possibility
that undulates between
joy and sadness,
peace and distress,
love and fear—
each potential moment
collapsing into reality.
This journey through duality requires energy
so you do not grow dim.
Do not look without
for what you already have within.
Focus not on the struggle,
but on the twinkling point of hope
that appears far in the distance—
at first a pinprick of light,
and then a rush and flash
of brilliance that does not blind,
that calls you into it
until all you experienced returns in union,
to oneness,
to wholeness,
your purpose complete.

Here

Fear
rose from the grave
and tried to convince you
you are merely human,
that you should be nervous
about your past,
that you should be anxious
about your present,
that you should worry
about your future,
that you should doubt
the love of anyone in your life.
Fear rose to tell you
love will leave you,
pain will come,
loss will overwhelm you,
and all you have will soon be swept away,
even your own self.
But I buried you, you protest,
What disregard has brought you back to life?
Fear replied,
I am the threat that never goes away,
and though you silence me,
I watch and wait for you to lose the sight
of who you are,

of why you are here,
and then I come to life.
Human nature is susceptible to fear,
for the body has a master called death.
But the soul does not—
it is the light that fear cannot put out.
The soul never dies.
You never die.
You are here for a purpose.
Retain this perspective,
and fear will not live in you
while you tread the earth.

Refinement

The thought returned
after you had
banished it beneath your conscious mind.
This was a resurrection
you never hoped for.
Panic followed,
as it always does,
when faced with what you thought you overcame.
I cannot fight this again, you said.
You can, the light replied,
do not give up.
I will walk with you
and catch you if you fall.
The soul keeps track of all experience,
all joy,
all sorrow,
all we feel and do.
Unsettled memories return
to show us where we need to grow.
They are a painful guide
aimed at the perfection of peace
and accomplishment,
like in reaching the mountaintop
and sighing in the view of the ineffable.
Although you may feel alone,

you are not.
No one is ever alone.
Do not fear the process of refinement,
but embrace it with acceptance and intent.
Allow it to reveal the inner shadow.
You will overcome once again.
And clarity will come,
like when water stills
and sunlight illuminates the ocean floor.

Waking

Let this morning be different.
Let the soft, golden light of sunrise
welcome you back
from your nighttime journey
through years of memory.
Let it speak hope to you
for the coming day,
possibility,
potential,
to remake and renew,
to explore and experience.
You are moving through your life.
If fear should rush upon you
for what you will encounter,
let it fade to gold
like surging light transforms the last of night.
You belong to the day.
Wake in the splendor
of new opportunity,
new purpose,
for traveling light cannot be bound or quelled,
but scatters darkness through eternity.
Now rise.

Brilliant

The fear of death
is foreign to the soul.
Light is life.
You are life.
When the soul blends in flesh
and walks the physical world,
it must confront the weight of human fear—
invisible like gravity
but more forceful in its pull.
The origin of fear
is in the end of physical life.
Human nature only knows
what it sees,
what it feels,
what it experiences.
It struggles to reconcile its own end,
because it cannot see past itself.
And so, it fears its inevitable demise.
But such is the way of this world.
The soul learns fear
only in the context of death.
Light is love.
You are love.
You will live,
and grow,

and expand your awareness,
ending but not ending,
moving through this outer darkness,
defining yourself
as shadow defines the edge of brilliant light.

Equilibrium

Not all you hold
is meant for you to keep.
Not all you touch
accepts the open hand.
Not all you love
returns the same to you.
The heart desires
to give itself in full
and searches with the energy
and curiosity of innocence
to find its reflection
in another.
And when it does,
it revels in the anticipated hope
of appeased longing,
corresponding desire,
requited investment,
fulfilled purpose—
the equilibrium of life and love.
The heart is made to
expand and contract
with the ebb and flow of possibility,
and then forever bond
in the eternal light of love.

Look Up Again

The nighttime sky
displays a billion stars
too vast for the human mind
to fathom
and hints that something greater must exist,
but even this could not move
or comfort you
in your grief,
in the immediate wake of a loss
so severe
you could only look down.
You knew anything was possible
in flesh on earth,
but you did not know this.
And so, you moved inward
to ease the brunt of pain
loss brings,
to give yourself time
to catch your breath
between thoughts of
why did this happen?
and
how can I continue on?
In the stillness of breath and memory,
the light spoke:

I loved you before time began,
before your light emerged to consciousness,
and you proceeded forth as light and life.
And I love you past the span of human breath,
when you return in the golden light of life.
Sorrow will pass.
Your soul will heal,
even from this.
And when you are ready,
love will help you stand
and look up again.

Release

Although you forgave the one
who hurt you,
the feelings that remain
try to convince you otherwise.
They accuse you with
But you are still angry,
you are still resentful,
you are still upset.
Doesn't this mean you have not forgiven?
No.
Forgiveness cancels the wrong
you hold against another,
releasing him from repayment
and removing any retaliation,
but it does not cancel the hurt.
Forgiveness is not contingent
on your state of recovery—
forgiveness is the first step of recovery.
It is not determined by how you feel
about the offense,
or by the work you now must do
to overcome the trauma of affliction.
Forgiveness does not remove
physical or emotional pain,
but lights the path to healing.

Anger is your righteous response
triggered by the shock
that another could do such a thing.
If you harbor anger or resentment,
it does not mean you have not forgiven,
but that you have not healed.
The severity of the offense
will determine the path and time it takes
to recover.
Human nature remembers
and recalls the moments of harm,
in attempt to deal with the aftermath,
in attempt to protect you from future harm.
The resurfacing of unprocessed trauma
reinvigorates the associated anger.
It is begging you to heal.
You can heal.
Take courage to process the trauma
to release its accompanying anger.
Shine light on the pain until it departs.
You are a light that darkness cannot overcome.

Insecurity

Insecurity
wrapped around you
like a blanket
and kept you from living unfettered,
unrestricted,
and free.
Early wounding taught you
emotional pain,
that you are not good enough,
that you are flawed,
that others will not accept you.
And so you moved
with the cloak of suspicion,
never showing your true self,
though you wished it were different.
The soul has the innate desire
to express itself,
to create,
to relate with others,
to give and receive.
It does not thrive behind a mask of fear.
You are good enough.
You are not flawed.
Whether others accept you or not
is out of your control,

and what is out of your control
is not worth apprehension or worry,
or letting it dictate your life.
Remember who you are.
Remember you are light in flesh
learning to illuminate the space
where possibility and expansion meet,
learning to overcome
the hardships and struggles
living brings.
You will grow and change,
and replace the blanket of insecurity
with a robe of confidence
and self-assurance,
ever moving, growing,
expressing, creating,
living.

Longing

When you decide to return,
I will be here.
I will not keep record
of any wrongs,
or hold against you
the reasons why you left.
I know the world is veiled in luring hues
and promises to grant your heart's longings,
to give meaning and purpose,
to define what you are worth.
But it will not.
It will take all you have to give,
then ask for more.
Desire is a flame to kindle carefully,
for its fire may rage too quickly
and leave you in darkness.
But I love you
and will always remind you
my hand is open and extended.
Love does not pull away,
but reaches patiently in expectation.
When you decide to return,
I will be here.

You Will Move On

If you should falter
and feel you cannot continue,
do not despair
at the difficulty you face,
for life is full of obstacles and strife.
You will move on.
If you should suffer
at the hands of another,
do not lose heart
or let such cruelty
define your past or commandeer your future.
You will move on.
If you should fear an end
because what is unknown
will not allow you
to see beyond the veil of human eyes,
still, you will move on.
You will move on
to where experience and resolution
form a single point.
The point will glisten like a faceted jewel
illuminated by a single light,
until its angles blend and merge as one
in the brilliance of understanding.
Only then will you know why
everything happened as it did.

Contentment

Frustration comes
when we do not receive
what we want.
Inner discontentment
casts its shadow
that reaches to the center of our being.
It dims the heart's light
enough to cause us to detect
the pain.
This is self-imposed.
An exterior catalyst
does not exist.
Instead, we project outside ourselves
desire that takes on its own existence,
becoming its own form.
When we fail to grasp it,
it produces in us feelings we abhor:
insecurity,
self-consciousness,
panic,
resentment.
Frustration is anger at unmet longing.
It is what we think should be
in place of what is.
The human self is never satisfied.

Do not spend your light
chasing illusions of desire.
But seek contentment
with who you are.
Self-fulfillment
does not come from the world of form.
Contentment is a light that heals the soul.

Decision

Hope always exists.
Darkness is never final,
whether you can see in it or not.
You have eyes
to observe the full spectrum of life,
but you must open them.
The heart can initiate or block potential.
Possibility is endless.
Time will pass
regardless of your joy or difficulty,
and you will wonder where it has gone.
The decision of positivity
is a spark that illuminates the invisible,
a guide through the world of shadow,
a beckoning of the promise of peace
like the first soft light of sunrise.

Gather Light

Do not worry about your
life.
But what does this mean?
Overcome
all the ways you think you are not
good enough,
beautiful enough,
smart enough,
bold enough.
Live as though
the ideals men chase and cherish
have no draw upon your soul.
You are not here to pursue
riches,
power,
fame,
or the accumulation of things.
Let go the desire to be loved
and that you are worth only
what another thinks of you.
The glorious sunset does not care
what the observer perceives.
Learn to love
the journey,
realizing the ending

is just a momentary pause
before beginning again.
It is while on the path
that you discover and grow,
stumble and recover,
gain new insight,
and find out what really matters.
Put aside all
fear
that prevents you from experience,
that convinces you
safety and stability
are better for you than
momentary discomfort.
Pain is a byproduct of progress
that fades when it is
no longer necessary.
Live intentionally.
Love unconditionally.
Continually seek experience.
Gather light.
Stand on the shore
and watch the sun come up again,
and again,
and again.

Anger

Anger is the discharge
of darker light
that stirs your soul.
Do not keep it spiraled inward,
but express it cautiously.
Anger has the potential
to be both a cleansing release
and an agent of suffering.
Careless anger hurts those in its path.
Anger results
when something disturbs
your equilibrium of peace—
the seat of all you hold as right and true.
Thought births anger
as you ponder
an offense to your soul.
But you don't have to let it rule you.
Anger is not justification for irresponsible actions.
Recognize its nature,
how it starts,
how it grows.
Learn to let it go
as certainly as it comes.
What is at first difficult
soon transforms into routine.
You are in control, not anger.

Passage

In the time it takes
your children to grow up,
you will have aged
more than you could comprehend
in your youth.
This will surprise you
because you did not have capacity
to understand it
while you were young.
While you were playing tag
and swinging on the jungle gym,
your parents aged
in real time before your eyes,
though you did not perceive it.
The passage of time
is the passage of life;
neither can exist without the other.
And where do you go from here?
You will deepen into years,
like how autumn blushes
in reds and oranges,
so beautiful,
and after the fall, rise up
for the final time,
and rise,

and rise,
and rise,
until you see through life,
and all your questions are answered,
and you return from where you came,
no more fractured,
yet weeping for the completion.

Design

The words struck your heart
like a poisoned arrow.
You absorbed the pain
that felt like a firestorm.
The toxin made its way
through your bloodstream,
but instead of killing you,
it paralyzed your self-confidence,
instilling fear
as a defense against further hurt.
This is hatred's design.
It cannot kill the body.
It targets the soul.
It seeks to elicit a withdrawal
from engaging the world.
But wisdom dispels hatred's power,
and understanding is the antidote
against hatred's venom.
Rise above the source of hatred.
Whatever desires to harm you
is below you,
for the origin of harm is fear,
and fear is the antithesis of love.
Do not fear the dimness in others
who use words as weapons.
Love conquers all.

Growth

Turn your thoughts toward growth.
Do not remain where you are
or rest in the comfort
of where you have been.
Life calls you to
rethink,
renew,
repurpose,
to change.
What you fear in change
is what you doubt about yourself—
Can I?
Will I?
What if?
A change in action first requires
a change in thought—
I can.
I will.
And then the movement of your brave soul,
to walk where you have never been,
to see what you have never seen.
Experience creates knowing,
and knowing marks the measure of your growth.
Expansion is a reward
for those who overcome the self.

Refocus

The world does not work
against you.
If trouble or difficulty
brings sorrow,
it's not as if the universe is angry
with what you did or failed to do.
If suffering or hardship
brings discouragement,
it's not as if your god is harming you
for the path you chose,
or how you chose to walk it.
Change your perspective.
Opportunity exists in pain.
Purpose exists in loss.
Consequence teaches wisdom
to those who will receive it.
Move past thoughts of fault
and victimization
into thoughts of potential.
Events only have the meaning
you give them.
The world works for you
in bringing aspects of yourself
to your attention.
Focus on the way forward

instead of on the way
that brought your present discomfort.
You have the ability to push through,
to persevere,
to reset your trajectory,
to redefine your future,
and then walk in newness of life.

Refining

Challenge is a blessing.
You do not always see it, though.
The pain and discomfort
color over the purpose,
which you cannot see
until you wipe away the dark hues.
So, you live with layers of
reds and blues,
not realizing the path of growth
curves between dense trees,
causing blind spots
which only resolve
when you have walked far enough around them.
Where you end
is never the same as where you begin,
regardless of your attitude.
Change your mind.
Change your thoughts.
Do not carry yesterday's negativity
that burdens your today.
You are going where you have not yet been,
so this means learning something new,
even if it is painful.
Do not cower at difficulty,
instead, embrace it

in the knowledge that
while the discomfort is temporary,
the gain is forever.
When gold is refined,
it hisses and pops as it melts down,
the impurities burning away.
And when it is complete,
its glow enthralls all who see it.

Present Light

Return to who you are
before life made a mess
of things,
before you went too far
and let your heart become
what you never could conceive.
In the time from there
to here,
the world deceived and destroyed you.
You left the door unlocked
to your inner sanctuary,
and the world stole
your sacred possessions.
But this is the lesson
your soul needed.
How else could you understand?
Return from here
to there,
return to the
you
who now has wisdom
from the bowel of depravity,
near insanity.
Return to where
the lilac blooms and paints the April air,

where
the sunlight tilts the flower's gentle petals,
where
the blue jay caws and the robin builds its nest,
where
time restores you in this present light.

Ocean

We have an ocean in us—
the movement of emotion of our souls,
at times wild and savage,
at other times tranquil and lulling.
Our lowest moments expose
the broken shells and sharp reefs
of our lives,
not knowing how to recover after loss,
how to handle pain, misfortune, tragedy.
We surge as strongly the other way
and lose ourselves in elation,
happiness, good fortune,
and the pleasure of inundation.
We gently sway back and forth
while holding one another,
or while standing and watching trees
or stars.
We carry others in our hearts,
our love the current of buoyancy.
We rage hard enough to destroy,
and calm ourselves enough to mirror light.
We are an expanse no one can see past,
beauty no one can fully take in,
depth no one can fathom,
desire that is never quenched.

Silence

Quiet your mind
amid the turmoil of life.
Perceive the world
between the dark and the light,
where right and wrong fade
and love becomes the standard
by which you set your compass.
You are not traveling by sight—
the world is but a passing phantom dream.
Neither do you move by sound—
what you hear is vibrational illusion.
Instead, sit in the seat of the heart—
the navigation center of the soul.
From here, you dream your dreams
and plot your course,
not based on others' wishes for you,
but on what you came to do.
Life is self-discovery
of all that was forgotten.
You will recover everything,
for nothing is ever lost,
only momentarily set aside.
In the stillness of thought
that sees through the veil,
you will remember the reason for

your purpose,
your life,
your light.
And then, through love,
you will expand into the gain of experience,
the same neither before nor after.
This is who you are.

Baseline

Do not let circumstances lessen your light.
The present moment of pain will pass,
and you will return to equilibrium,
to the evenness of emotion
that allows you to see
the potential good to come.
You undulate between
happiness and sadness,
passion and apathy,
hopefulness and discouragement.
This oscillation gives you perspective
of the full spectrum of experience.
You move with strengthening grace
between the crest and trough,
though you may not perceive it.
Just as you, by nature, descend into hardship,
so you, by nature, must also ascend.
Circumstances change,
as they always must,
so do not let the present difficulty
convince you to give up,
or that you are unworthy.
You will rise.
You will overcome.
And you will see the gain
when you return to baseline.

Light Eternal

We thrash and yearn
in the ignorance of darkness,
not knowing what sits
outside our limited perspective.
It's not until we notice piercing light
that our soul discovers the veil
that blocks our sight,
that hides the truth
of who we are,
from where we have come,
and why.
We don't understand the reason
for why we move in such a hindered way,
and our inherent longing
reinforces curiosity.
Light cannot pass out of existence,
it can only be blocked for a time.
And so, the veil must lift.
And so, we must burst forth,
not as a result of human effort,
but by the truth of our immortal home
that beckons us to see with reborn eyes,
to rediscover what we left, and more,
to bring us back to our eternal light.

Don't Quit

Don't quit, change course.
If it's not working, try something else.
Quitting forfeits all momentum
previous attempts earned.
What if you were one more try from success?
You can endure the pain,
the frustration.
You will do what you intend.
Don't quit, rethink what you are doing.
Everything is conquerable.
What if you were a day away from victory,
or an hour, or a minute?
The only way to know
is to push to accomplishment or failure.
And if you fail,
begin again.
Failure is the unexpected teacher
who freely grants wisdom,
unless you give up,
then it is your unmerciful master.
Don't quit, persevere.
The end result will prove
the worth of the endeavor.
Everything is possible.

Discovery

Regardless of what you experience
here,
you are moving forward.
You are not required
to figure everything out,
or conform to what another calls success.
Worth is not found in accomplishment,
but in existence.
Beauty is not revealed by comparison,
but by acknowledgement.
All of life is but a coming forth,
like the budding flower,
or the spring that never ends.
Life is a discovery,
a learning how to look,
how to see,
how to live.
Do not waste your time in judgment
of yourself or others—
acceptance is the light that shows the path.
Life is an unfolding
of purpose,
of progress,
of love.

Joy

We seek what pleases us,
for pleasure brings a sense of fulfillment.
We will endure pain
if we can find joy in the payoff.
Desire for joy is innate to humanity.
In joy, we feel a sense of well-being,
for ourselves,
for others,
for the world.
Joy brings a sense of satisfaction
to the soul,
for reason and purpose hide within it.
Joy is the wish for wellness realized,
the overflow of the heart
when it acknowledges truth,
the confirmation of happiness
that cannot be contained.
Joy leaves behind
light for the path of life,
that others may follow
and find its treasure.

Within

You struggled with right and wrong
all your life
because you looked outside yourself
for something to guide you,
to tell you what to do,
to tell you what to think.
You did not know the truth
that sat within your own soul,
waiting for you to discover.
You went here and there,
looking for this and that,
the whole time watching every step
so you did not
cross a line,
or break a rule.
You lost yourself in the traditions of men,
ever searching for the highest version
of right,
and binding yourself to it,
grasping it like it was life itself,
and this from fear.
You did not know
it was merely human thought forms,
born from human longing,
from human forgetting,

ascribing the highest conceivable extreme
of moral duality
to define God itself.
How could you have known?
It wasn't until the inevitable falter
that you understood.
Falling broke the spell
that you are judged by standards
no human can keep,
that God is defined
by an illusory world's paradigms,
that motivation and pressure from fear
are of the light.
And then you finally looked within,
realizing all you were searching for
was hiding behind the wall of yourself.
Who am I? you asked.
The light answered, *You are whole,*
you are worthy,
you are enough,
you are light,
you are love,
you are.

Unknown

We fear the unknown
out of the instinct of
self-preservation.
We are afraid of
what we do not understand,
that it may have the power
to harm us,
or to take from us.
We inspect,
measure,
weigh,
and dissect,
to appease our suspicion
that a thing unknown
is a thing unwelcome.
Second-hand knowledge
is not good enough;
we must see for ourselves.
Experience proves uncertainty,
and is the cure-all for ignorance.
The unknown keeps us ever vigilant,
and calls us
to explore,
to discover,
to risk finding out,
perhaps to learn to love before we fear.

Last Light

We long for an ending
when we are tired from the journey,
the heart now weary
from tribulation,
from struggle,
from desire of accomplishment.
We put all our effort
into doing what we think will please us.
Life is a progression of
discovering and pursuing pleasure,
a never-ending quest for satisfaction.
But eventually we learn
that we do not gain happiness
from achievement or its pursuit.
Fortunate is the one who
wearies from his endeavors,
for when he rests from his labor,
he will find true fulfillment.
He can live,
not in the hope of some future reward,
but in the peace that presence brings,
that the self is whole,
not lacking.
His peace is a solemn and muted glow,
like the last of evening light.

Perfection

Life continues,
even after loss.
The difficulty decreases
as time passes.
But it was the heart
you struggled with.
It was the remembrance
of moments shared,
of happiness and sadness,
joy and struggle.
You savored the good
but repudiated the bad.
Loss forced you to let go,
your hands unable to grasp,
except for regret,
which you could not shake off.
But you are human,
and human life is not a scripted act
that only has positive scenes.
You can learn to live through hardship,
to push past your fault or guilt,
because you are human,
only for a time,
a time to experience,
to learn,

to grow.
Perfection is not flawless living,
but the ability to embody
both good and bad
and incorporate them
into the growth of your soul.

Robin

Stop worrying.
You are not in control.
Life will flow as it will,
beyond your ability to understand.
Its purpose hides behind
the formation of what is physical.
Its reason was established
before you made your way into flesh.
Uncertainty is a necessary part
of this world.
Why should you give it control
over how you feel,
what you think,
and who you are?
You imagine the worst
in the hope of being able to better handle it,
your thoughts now a defense
against what you do not want to experience.
But this is not living.
Stop worrying.
Acknowledge the potential,
but then let it go.
Why would you ruminate on
what may never happen?
Worry steals joy and peace.

Focus on what is good and healthy.
Become the positive in life,
ever holding its potential in view,
like how the robin lives
to sing in the morning,
not wasting its time worrying
if the night will ever pass.

Illusion

Life is a never-ending incorporation of experience.
We live for the unfolding of events,
for purpose played out,
each hour a new chapter
in the reason for existence.
Categorize it as you will—
each moment your interpretation
and assigning of meaning:
this was good;
that was bad.
But such reasoning misses the purpose.
You are not here to judge endlessly
between right and wrong,
and your association with it,
and whether others understand it.
You will find happiness
when you let what is to be.
Do not let the duality of this world
push you back and forth,
or fool you into thinking
the essence of life is
based on such polarization.
You are already whole.
You already know the way of love.
Find the ancient way within yourself,
then walk the path that leads through the illusion.

Brighten

The way forward
includes coming to terms with yourself,
what you said and did.
Anger and frustration
are temporary states you go through
before you accept your actions.
Acceptance is the stone that slays the giant.
It gives insight into the
why
of how you chose to move.
It clears the path of thorns
that grew from the choices you made.
This is how healing begins.
Acceptance opens the door
to see reason and purpose,
not only of past mistakes,
but of future traveling.
You are light.
You are the only one who can dim yourself.
And so, you are the only one
who can brighten yourself.
Choose the lighted way,
for darkness cannot infringe
on the way forward.
You will find your way.

Captured

Moving forward was never the problem—
it was looking back.
You gave the past the power
to control where you placed your feet—
go here, don't go there,
watch your step.
It was the feelings
the memories produced,
as if you were living them again:
insecurity,
loneliness,
shame,
regret.
You are only prisoner
to the bars you choose to stand behind,
captured.
But you do not have to replay the memories
as some sort of penance.
You do not owe the present
a payment from the past,
a guilt offering,
a sacrifice.
Let the past die.
After you have mourned yesterday's failures,
you may look toward tomorrow,

where the soul is free to try again,
to explore,
to fail again if it must,
all in the knowledge that
to live is to learn,
to grow,
to change.
Walk by your present light.

Creation

Thoughts of the past or future
do not matter.
The present moment lights the forward way.
Can you travel backward in time
and change what you said or did,
or how you felt about it?
Then why give it power
to scare you,
to intimidate you,
to make you fear that you have failed in life?
The past disappears
like the sun beneath the horizon.
Only your memory can rewind it.
Let it fade.
Or, can you travel forward in time
and align the pieces
to bring forth your deepest desires?
Then why give it power
to worry you,
to cause alarm,
to make you fear that you will not be happy?
The future is an illusion
of the potential of possible moments.
It does not exist.
The present moment is your true reality.

Past and future are only figments of
memory and imagination—
the torture of where you have been,
and the anxiety of where you want to be.
So, live now, in the present.
You have the ability to change,
to learn,
to grow.
Every moment is creation.

On Desire

Desire is fire in the soul.
Kindle it wisely,
or it may burn out of control.
The same fire that warms you
can also consume you.
Why do you want what you want?
From where does desire spring?
You perceive some sort of lack
in your innermost being,
from the place where you derive worth.
All lack is pain, the uncomfortable fear
of not being enough, of not having enough.
Lack threatens survival.
Human nature fights to live
and produces a response to conquer lack—
this stirs desire.
True need is the wellspring of healthy desire.
But desire can be dangerous
when you apply it to wants
that are based on perceived self-worth.
Your worth is not linked to survival
or accomplishment.
You are worthy because of who you are,
and who you are never lacks anything.
Peace is an acceptance of your inner light.
To be is the culmination of worth.

Transcend

To fear is to be human
in this transitory world
where we embrace survival
as the foundation for living.
Fear is inherent in the design
where one is tasked to stay alive,
and forced to fight, flee, or be killed.
At first convinced that this is all there is,
we rely upon our human instincts
in all we do and think,
putting ourselves first
to ensure survival.
What horrors has this primal drive produced.
We kill one other,
malign one another,
make fun of and criticize one another,
we suppress, intimidate,
take advantage of and abuse
one another.
Hatred is born from the fear
for our own survival.
Only when we awaken to the truth
that this reality is not our home,
that our beginning was not a birth in flesh,
that we are more than what this dim light shows,

do we understand why we are here,
and why the world is as it is.
And only then can we transcend
the nature that we willingly took on,
to fight, to struggle,
to learn, to grow,
to face the trial of this dim existence,
to find again the love that conquers fear.

Downpour

Trauma is the hardest part of life.
It surprises you,
like being caught in a downpour
you did not see coming,
then not knowing which way to turn
to find shelter.
It forces you to fight or flee,
to preserve your life.
Trauma is destructive
because it is violence to your well-being.
It impacts the way you see others,
and yourself.
It is an unwelcome teacher
of the darker way of this world.
But you are not darkness.
The remains of others' actions
belong to them,
not you.
Do not hold on to them.
Though you may struggle to let them go,
hope exists.
Hope lives in the realization
that you are not defined by other's harm,
that you have power to move forward,
to move beyond,

becoming stronger than you were before.
The downpour never lasts forever,
and wet clothes always dry.
The sun comes back out
and warms the world.

The Regrettable

Do not think you have wasted years,
even in the regrettable.
You are human.
To live is to learn.
To learn is to grow.
To grow is to change.
Change brings opportunity for understanding,
not of what you should
or should not have done,
but of what you did.
The thought is the rumination of desire,
the action is the culmination.
No waste exists in action,
for it is how you chose to move forward.
You will continue to move forward.
All life is moving forward.
The meaning you ascribe
to your movement may change
in the passage of time.
Understanding may change.
Do not be so hard on yourself.

Paradigm

There is no winning or losing.
You are not here
in competition
as if in a game
where the goal is to have more
than someone else.
Would you have won
if by the end
you had an abundance of
happiness, fulfillment, material things,
or fame, respect, wealth, relationships?
And would you have lost
if by the end
you were disgraced, poor, pitiful,
or lost, broken, failed, hated, angry?
To ascribe such a paradigm to your time here
is to misunderstand your life.
To judge yourself on such parameters
is to subvert the reason
why you came.
You are here to live.
What you interpret as winning or losing
is neither.
You are here to move
through the full spectrum of available light

and color your soul with life's potential,
with life's experience.
This is your growth.
This is your gain.
This is your reason for moving.

Visible Light

Do not awaken the soul
too soon.
Give yourself time to live
blindly to the light that hides within.
For it is in the dark unawareness
that you may learn to
stumble,
struggle,
endure,
and overcome.
This is why you are here.
Far from the golden realm of light,
the opportunity exists
to live in such a way that tests your soul,
where passion and desire
emerge to fight the fear survival brings.
Death is a temporary enemy
that pursues and pushes you to live.
Tragedy and loss
are not what they seem;
they are not one-sided.
When you have taken in enough of life,
the light within will slowly grow
and bring awareness to your inner self—
understanding,

perspective,
surprise,
joy,
compassion for the decisions you made
in the time you have been alive,
and love that transcends
the realm of visible light.

Seasons

Only when summer nears the end,
when it cools down,
are you ready to let go.
It's the passing of the season
that you saw through
from its beginning
to where you now stand.
Endings feel different from beginnings.
When you begin, the world is new.
You look forward with unbridled expectation
of all you hope to experience.
The light is bright and crisp
and fills you with the hope of day.
When the end nears,
the light changes.
What was golden in the morning
is again golden in the evening,
though richer and deeper now in hue.
It carries the weight of experience,
the weight of life lived
with all of its joy and drama,
happiness and sadness,
pain and pleasure.
Letting go
is an art you are forced to learn,

for seasons never last forever,
though you may want them to.
Midway through, when you have been
lost in the recollection living brings,
does it cross your mind that this will end,
as all things do,
as all things must,
in a transitory world
where passing time insists you move ahead.
Embrace and revel in the golden light,
with the insight of what is to come,
an ending that is not an ending,
but another beginning.

Grow

Learning to give
what you were never given
takes courage
to move beyond
what you think you are capable of.
Grow.
Push the boundary
of where you think you can go.
The first step only requires
a decision to act.
Do not let what is unfamiliar
frighten you
or cause you to pause in hesitation.
Do not let questions
of why you were never taught
stir in you disappointment or helplessness.
No one is at fault.
Others have done the best they could
for you.
Take ownership of how you walk
and what you want to achieve.
Life is a teacher
that never stops suggesting
ways in which you can change.
Allow its instruction

and it will show you the way forward.
You have it in you to transform,
to be the person you want to be,
in how you relate with others
and even yourself.
When you have grown
and become what you previously lacked,
look back and note the change.
From there, nothing is impossible.

Awareness

Far past the boundary
of who you think you are,
a light shines brighter
than you could ever imagine
in flesh.
Far beyond all
pain,
pleasure,
joy,
or sadness,
a single constant brilliance emanates
and radiates through universal space.
You cannot tell
if it is moving or standing still.
You cannot tell
where you end
and the light begins.
The light creates the stage
upon which you dance,
moment to moment,
experience to experience.
Purpose comes from
how you choose to interpret
your movement.
You will see what you will see,

regardless of what others perceive.
You will do what you will do,
regardless of what others do.
Life belongs to you,
for it exists through you.
But why? you ask.
The light replied,
So you may come to the awareness
that surpasses all things,
whether past, present, or future,
that sees through what was, is, or will be,
that understands its part
in what is greater than its own self,
and the necessity of illusion
in this bringing forth.

December

No one knows what to give or take with leaving,
or what they should have said
or wanted to
in memory of you.
The first snowfall was brief and comforting,
and turned the grass
a lighter shade of green
in that December scene.
The waning sun was cruel and unforgiving,
unwilling to allow
the salve in grief
and utter disbelief.
Nature is immutable, uncaring,
posing as the sovereignty of god
to all the hearts it trod.
And human nature follows with it,
binding the soul that lives
within its flesh enclave,
momentarily enslaved,
willingly depraved,
struggling to transcend,
that in losing you,
no one knows what to give or take with leaving.

Opportunity

You cannot lose.
So do not fear the thought.
Life will tempt you with
worry and anxiety,
but you have the power
to rise from the ash.
Do not let the opportunity pass,
but reach out your hand
and grasp the moment.
If you willingly let it slip away,
you may look back with remorse
on what you did not strive to manifest.
You can do all you desire.
By will, you bring image into form.
If you should fail by effort,
do not mourn what you could not do,
for success does not always prove purpose.
Instead, reset your sight
and try again.
Losing is not the enemy you make it,
as if it holds the authority
to declare a finality.
Though a situation may seek to paralyze you,
it is only a passing moment.
You are the one in control.

You decide whether to surrender or fight.
You cannot lose.
So stand and take the chance.
Life will bring before you
prospect and possibility,
and you have the power
to forge your reality.

Between

The time for flowers is over.
The light is dimming.
Noon has lost its power
to spur the world to growth.
This is the way of things.
Always the waxing and the waning,
the rising and the falling,
the arrival and the leaving.
The time between matters most.
We ascribe meaning
to beginnings and endings
based on our own experience of the world.
No one can tell you what to believe.
But why should the bookends of life
hold more of an emotional impact
than the contents of its pages?
It's the drama of coming and going.
We lose ourselves in living,
so much that it becomes mundane,
that we lose sight
of the beauty in one another,
of the world,
of what we came to experience,
of how we change and grow.
Living seeks its meaning in the light,

in the long day,
in this in-between,
where free will and predestination
blend to push and guide us on our way.
All of life is a rejoicing.

Moment

This journey is but a moment,
a plunge in deep water
where we hold our breath
and eventually come back up to breathe.
The time without air
provides the stress we seek
to press and form our will and understanding.
All longings in life
spring from desires for
happiness,
peace,
comfort,
and security.
We want to live in alignment
with what is natural to our being,
though we immerse into the unnatural
while on this journey.
And so pain and suffering must exist.
A streak of light from up above
can penetrate this depth
and remind us of our home,
illuminating the memory
of a place forgotten,
ever remaining,
ever golden.

Choose

Take strength and run.
Why would you sit in suffering?
The moment is meant to pass,
so do not extend its length
by accepting the lie it tells you.
Will you live in fear,
or will you live in love?
You must choose between the two.
You come from love—
this is your nature.
Fear can only exist
in the absence
or blurring of love,
in the obscuring of yourself.
The world is meant to test your soul
that lives in flesh,
always presenting the choice
that will bind or free you.
Expansion comes from moving through the dark.
Experience drips wisdom
that is the light of life,
for you
and for those who come after.
You know nothing
until you have experienced it.

The light will lead you out of fear,
but you must choose to follow.
Love will lead you back to yourself,
through yourself,
until all you see is the golden outline
of your brilliant soul
against this dense reality.

Slower Light

When you cannot face the day,
when you cannot take anymore
of what life brings,
I see you.
Life was once a dream
of imagined potential
that promised to renew you
in the coming forth,
to build you,
to move you to a higher consciousness.
But you did not know the pain
it would take to accomplish this.
And in this pain,
the light of life grows dim
as you struggle to understand its reason.
Doubt is where dim sight leads,
as it must,
for truth hides in the guise of slower light.
Do not give up.
Do not give in.
Night has a purpose,
but its darkness is not eternal
and must give way to the brightening.
And in your passing through,
I see you.

Descending

The descent is but a dream
from which you cannot awaken.
You wanted it this way.
The drop at first is startling,
the heaviness,
the weight of a million years of evolution
to give you opportunity
to see,
to feel,
to love.
What was it you were expecting?
Whatever it was,
it vanished from your memory
like a ghost that disappears before your eyes.
The forgetting clears the way for you to move.
Without this,
you would remember the golden shore,
and lose the sense of risk that living brings.
For now, live.
Revel in the struggle to survive.
You are forever loved.
If you seek to peer through the veil,
you may get a glimpse of golden light.
But only when your slumber runs its course
will you begin to stir.

The light will gently whisper in your ear,
Return to me,
awaken from your dream,
and see again my face,
my love,
this light.

Unveiled

Life will end.
It must.
There's no fighting it.
The harder you try to understand it
from this side of the illusion,
the harder it is to accept,
and the more absurd it becomes
that this is the way things should be.
This is because death
is the antithesis of life,
inconceivable to the immortal soul
until it takes on flesh.
But you must accept it.
What is life, anyway?—
a string of moments
experienced from a single point
of consciousness,
clothed in physical duality
with the absence of remembrance?
You must overcome
the fear of the inevitable,
the fear of finality,
the fear that your existence ends.
Death is an illusory end
in a life that was never meant to be permanent.

You are just passing through,
as all are just passing through.
You know this in the depth of your soul.
You grieve
from the perspective of your humanity,
for you are human.
But that grief will turn to joy
when the world around you fades to faster light,
and you return to the wholeness that is life,
the illusion dissolved,
the crown of experience upon your head,
the restoration of all things,
the reunion of all whom you loved
and who loved you,
and the light,
yes, the light,
forever golden in your eyes.

Ascent

You start by forgetting
all you know
and who you have become.
Far from the realm
that you call home,
the golden light is now a faded dream.
The work of physicality
demands you give your full attention.
For it is here you learn and grow,
explore and discover,
love and are loved.
The light here is a dense shadow
bent downward,
yet it still holds within itself
the essence of its origin,
for nothing can exist
apart from the one from which it came.
Your individuality is an illusion
of separation,
a divine decree by which you live and move.
Your years in the innocence of ignorance
are when you learn the most,
for it is here that you run blindly
to test the nature of your precious soul,
to experience life without hindrance

of the knowledge of who you really are.
The world is for you,
providing good and bad,
right and wrong,
black and white,
to give you opportunity for everything.
Not until youth grows to maturity
will the soul question its nature.
What am I?
Who am I?
And from there, each question
is a tug on the veil,
an attempt to disclose the illusion
you so willfully embraced,
but it will never give up its secret,
not until you have come to completion.
And when you have finished your work,
and done what you came here to do,
the veil will lift,
and you will begin the ascent,
the journey to awaken to the truth
of all you laid aside,
and from where you have come.
In passing through a darkness, you will see,
and memory will once again return,
a flash of surprise,
a flood of golden light,
the brilliance of a never-ending life.

Union

Come back to me.
When memory cannot recall
all you have been,
all you are.
You will return
when the amber wave of light
has given its final warmth,
when the hummingbird
has spent its final September day
before the dimming sun
triggers its long migration home.
All your thoughts of the light
were elusive as a dream
that faded upon waking,
remembering only
the slightest feeling of presence.
You sensed it was there,
but you never knew for sure.
Life is cruel
in that its very source
hides its face beneath the waterline,
blurry though you stare intently,
the wind and waves
rippling and warping its image.
Or was that just your reflection?

Time here is both
triumph and burden.
Duality soothes and scorches the soul.
Though purpose was a crown you strived to grasp,
in the end it was love
that mattered.
Love is your home.
Love illuminates all
within and without.
The light remembers where you have been,
and where you began.
And so, the light will say again,
Come back to me.

After

All your life was a movement toward light,
an unknown destination
that called to you,
though you did not know why.
How had I forgotten? you asked.
Life was like being under water
but still breathing,
going where you wanted
but only slower.
It fascinated and thrilled you
with its highs,
and traumatized and scared you
with its lows.
Purpose hovered in the background,
though you could not see its brushstrokes.
In all your movement,
you wondered if a hidden hand
was guiding and protecting you.
Or was it just coincidence and chance?
A master never shows you how he works.
You experienced good and bad
with the full force of emotion
each situation conjured in you,
for this is the human way.
You embraced the richness that is life,

that is found in each passing moment,
each a varied hue and intensity,
creating a kaleidoscope
of love, hate,
joy, sorrow,
pleasure, pain.
And now, those jewels
are all your gain.
What beauty does the next horizon hold?

A Movement of Light

I will echoed through the timeless void
before it slowed enough
to take a form.
Its intention was unparalleled
and pregnant with eternal possibility—
the highest joy,
the lowest sorrow,
fortune and tragedy—
within the brush mark of a single stroke.
To individuate the inseparable
required an illusion
so remarkable
that even the divine could lose itself
within itself—
the momentary chaos of a dream
where unknown potential
was the triumph of its masterpiece.
Nothing can exist apart from that
from which it came;
all must find its source within the one
who brought it forth.
In the attempt to understand the light,
you wondered if its brilliance
was its only possible manifestation,
or if it could have taken the nature

of something different,
maybe a deep blue mist,
or perhaps a thing more ineffable,
if even a thing at all,
unimaginable until it showed you its face.
But it would never show you its face.
You lived on earth
as a human being,
driven by the instinct to survive
within the stark illusion
that nothing more exists,
except what your hands could touch.
You searched for the light
through reason, religion,
in nature, and in your children's eyes.
You finally understood
that you would never find it here,
enough to prove its existence
in this world,
and that the point was not to unveil its essence,
but to separate from it
for your own self-discovery.
The purpose was not to eliminate doubt and uncertainty,
but to live in illusive abandonment.
Fear is foreign to the golden realm,
so fear is foreign to the soul.
But fear drives expansion.
Fear grows the farther you travel from the light.
And so fear is in the forgetting,

in the unawareness
of the true essence of yourself
that hides in flesh,
in the unawareness
of the light
that hides in everything,
even yourself.
All is one,
for all has come from one,
a never-ending fractalized expression,
a reverie of reality
in a mask of physicality,
an experience of separation
within the unity of all that is.
What is the self?
You wondered about its nature,
and if its essence
is truly singular
or something more.
Far past the edge of human sight,
a web of light
connects billions of souls,
immense, eternal,
forever shining.
And farther still
a greater light glitters and gleams,
a brilliance of infinite souls,
from which we set out
and to which we return,

the beginning and the ending,
a home forgotten
in the glory of the journey,
the final frontier,
the self remembered,
the self together,
the self of the one.
Dreams are meant to end.
They do not last forever,
despite their joy or terror.
And while you dream,
your awareness is singular,
lost in the world of temporary illusion,
unaware of the truth
of the momentary state of being,
until you awaken,
and a higher sense of reality returns.
And like all dreams,
this one will end, too.
Only love transcends the distance
you think you have traveled,
from that which is,
to that which is to be,
to that which has always been.
Love is the light that imbues all things,
that gives and sustains all life.
A streak of light shot out
from the infinite oneness.
And though the golden light dimmed

from its sight,
it carried its essence.
It gave and took what it was meant to,
and did all it intended to do.
In the end, it returned
and stood again upon the golden shore,
in the full remembrance of love,
in the full recollection of its being,
greater now than when it first departed,
a deeper hue of gold,
a brighter brilliance of essence,
enhancing the singularity of the one,
forever golden,
forever eternal,
forever love.
You are a movement of light.

Thematic Subject Index

The poems in this book contain a variety of themes. Sometimes, a single poem will touch on multiple themes. The following subject index lists out some of the more major themes and highlights where they are more prominently featured.

Change: 25, 64, 95

Death: 27, 28, 31, 34, 41, 100, 117

Encouragement: 15, 22, 24, 30, 40, 51, 55, 62, 73, 88, 107, 114

Fear: 28, 36, 41, 78, 82

Forgiveness: 18, 32, 46

Grief: 27, 31, 44, 106, 118

Growth: 22, 38, 61, 64, 102

Healing: 17, 20, 85

Hope: 54

Human Nature: 17, 32, 37, 43, 46, 48, 52, 57, 68, 75, 90, 91

Identity: 30, 49, 66, 74, 76, 104, 112, 120, 125

The light speaking: 32, 38, 44, 76, 104, 114, 115, 121, 125

Loss: 20, 34, 44, 80

Love: 43, 50, 112

Origins: 21, 120, 121, 125

Purpose of life: 16, 30, 35, 58, 69, 72, 74, 84, 91, 96, 98, 109, 111, 115, 118, 119, 121, 123, 125

Recovery: 66, 71, 86

Trauma: 32, 60, 93

About the Author

Keith Wrassmann holds the degrees of MA in Creative Writing: Poetry from Miami University (Oxford, OH) and MDiv in Theology from Cincinnati Christian University, where he also won the Theological Studies Award. He lives in the greater Cincinnati, Ohio area with his wife and children.

Visit www.keithwrassmann.com for more.

www.ingramcontent.com/pod-product-compliance
Lightning Source LLC
Chambersburg PA
CBHW051807040426
42446CB00007B/565